WARS THAT CHANGED AMERICAN HISTORY

The American Revolution

Deborah DeFord

WORLD ALMANAC® LIBRARY

Please visit our Web site at: www.garethstevens.com
For a free color catalog describing World Almanac® Library's list of high-quality books
and multimedia programs, call 1-800-848-2929 (USA) or 1-800-387-3178 (Canada).
World Almanac® Library's fax: (414) 332-3567

Library of Congress Catalog-in-Publication Data

DeFord, Deborah H.
  The American Revolution / by Deborah DeFord. — North American ed.
     p. cm. — (Wars that changed American history)
  Includes bibliographical references and index.
  ISBN-10: 0-8368-7289-4 – ISBN-13: 978-0-8368-7289-7 (lib. bdg.)
  ISBN-10: 0-8368-7298-3 – ISBN-13: 978-0-8368-7289-9 (softcover)
  1. United States—History—Revolution, 1775-1783—Juvenile literature.
  I. Title. II. Series.
  E208.D46   2007
  973.3—dc22   2006011588

First published in 2007 by
World Almanac® Library
A Member of the WRC Media Family of Companies
330 West Olive Street, Suite 100
Milwaukee, WI 53212 USA

Copyright © 2007 by World Almanac® Library.

A Creative Media Applications, Inc. Production
Design and Production: Alan Barnett, Inc.
Editor: Susan Madoff
Copy Editor: Laurie Lieb
Proofreader: Lynne Arany
Indexer: Nara Wood
World Almanac® Library editorial direction: Mark J. Sachner
World Almanac® Library editor: Leifa Butrick
World Almanac® Library art direction: Tammy West
World Almanac® Library production: Jessica Morris

Picture credits: cover photo: The Granger Collection; The Library of Congress: pages 5, 8, 15, 16, 20, 21, 28, 30, 34, 38; New York Public Library, Astor, Lenox and Tilden Foundations: pages 11, 19, 26, 27; Northwind Pictures Archives: pages 12, 25, 29, 31, 39, 41; Bridgeman Art Library: pages 13, 36; maps courtesy of Ortelius Design

Printed in the United States of America

1 2 3 4 5 6 7 8 9 10 09 08 07 06

Table of Contents

Cover: British General Charles Cornwallis (in red uniform) meets with Continental Army General George Washington and the commander of the French force, Comte de Rochambeau, to formally surrender on October 19, 1781, ending the Revolutionary War and recognizing the independence of the American colonies and the newly formed United States of America.

INTRODUCTION

From the time when America declared its independence in the 1700s to the present, every war in which Americans have fought has been a turning point in the nation's history. All of the major wars of American history have been bloody, and all of them have brought tragic loss of life. Some of them have been credited with great results, while others partly or entirely failed to achieve their goals. Some of them were widely supported; others were controversial and exposed deep divisions within the American people. None will ever be forgotten.

The American Revolution created a new type of nation based on the idea that the government should serve the people. As a result of the Mexican-American War, the young country expanded dramatically. Controversy over slavery in the new territory stoked the broader controversy between Northern and Southern states over the slavery issue and powers of state governments versus the federal government. When the slave states seceded, President Abraham Lincoln led the Union into a war against the Confederacy—the Civil War—that reunited a divided nation and ended slavery.

▼ Wars have shaped the history of the United States of America since the nation was founded in 1776. Conflict in this millennium continues to alter the decisions the government makes and the role the United States plays on the world stage.

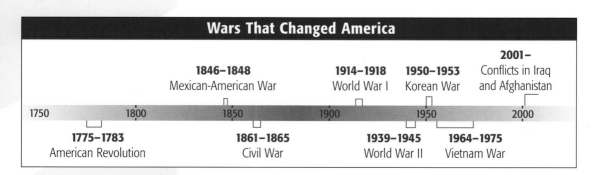

Wars That Changed America

| 1775–1783 American Revolution | 1846–1848 Mexican-American War | 1861–1865 Civil War | 1914–1918 World War I | 1939–1945 World War II | 1950–1953 Korean War | 1964–1975 Vietnam War | 2001– Conflicts in Iraq and Afghanistan |

1750 · 1800 · 1850 · 1900 · 1950 · 2000

The American Revolution

The roles that the United States played in World War I and World War II helped transform the country into a major world power. In both these wars, the entry of the United States helped turn the tide of the war.

Later in the twentieth century, the United States engaged in a Cold War rivalry with the Soviet Union. During this time, the United States fought two wars to prevent the spread of communism. The Korean War essentially ended in a stalemate, and after years of combat in the Vietnam War, the United States withdrew. Both claimed great numbers of American lives, and following its defeat in Vietnam, the United States became more cautious in its use of military force.

That trend changed when the United States led the war that drove invading Iraqi forces from Kuwait in 1990. After the al-Qaeda terrorist attacks of September 11, 2001, the United States again led a war, this time against Afghanistan, which was sheltering al-Qaeda. About two years later, the United States led the invasion that toppled Iraq's dictatorship.

In this book, readers will learn about the evolution of American independence and how a small group of colonies banded together to improbably defeat an empire that was both shortsighted in its political maneuverings and overconfident about its military strength. The American Revolution brought about the very existence of the United States of America and influenced the way the nation's citizens have viewed its place in the world ever since the 1700s.

▲ Declaration of Independence, *by John Trumbull, currently hangs in the U.S. Capitol. The painting dramatizes the signing of the Declaration of Independence in 1776. John Hancock is seated at the table. Across from him are (left to right) John Adams, Roger Sherman, Robert R. Livingston, Thomas Jefferson, and Benjamin Franklin. Although fifty-six men signed the declaration, fifteen of the signers are not represented in this painting. In addition, the likenesses of four men who were in the room when the document was adopted (George Clinton, Robert R. Livingston, Thomas Willing, and John Dickinson) but did not sign it are included.*

CHAPTER 1

On the Road to Revolution

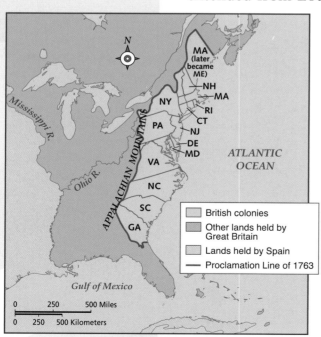

▼ *This map illustrates the Proclamation Line of 1763 in red. The line restricted colonists from settling beyond the Appalachian Mountains in order to avoid angering Native Americans living on that land. The British believed they could avoid future violence with the Indians in the area, but colonists were angered by what they believed was a restriction of their rights.*

British colonies

Other lands held by Great Britain

Lands held by Spain

— Proclamation Line of 1763

In the mid-1700s, North America was home to an ever-growing number of European immigrants and their descendants. Most of these colonists came from Great Britain. Although many had spent their entire life in America, they still considered themselves British **citizens** and subjects of the British king, George III.

North America, meanwhile, was at the center of a great contest. Britain claimed much of the eastern seaboard and parts of what would become present-day Canada. France claimed territory that extended from Louisbourg, Nova Scotia, in the north to New Orleans, Louisiana, in the south and stretched far west of the Appalachian Mountains. Spain settled Florida and parts of the southwest. Both Britain and France claimed ownership of the land of the Ohio River valley. Soon, they would fight a war over this territory, changing the future of America and forcing the colonists to decide how they wished to govern and be governed.

The American Revolution

Native Peoples

From the Europeans' first arrival in North America, they had encountered Native American nations and tribes. Different Native languages were spoken in every part of the land, and Indians worshipped according to their own varied beliefs. They hunted, fished, and farmed the land. Although they did not believe in owning land as Europeans did, the Indian nations claimed specific territories as their traditional homelands.

In some regions, Europeans and Indians became friends and agreed to a cooperative relationship. The Native people soon discovered, though, that friendships did not guarantee that their land and lives would be respected by the newcomers. Europeans, meanwhile, learned that the Native Americans could be deadly enemies.

The French made the Native people their **allies** more easily than the English. France settled its territory sparsely, leaving much of the Indian territory open. Britain's colonists, however, arrived in rapidly increasing numbers and built towns and farms. While the French traded with the Indians for furs and rewarded their friendship with gifts of guns and other goods, the English pushed the Native people off their traditional lands.

Early Colonial Wars

From the end of the 1600s to the mid-1700s, three major conflicts broke out in Europe, principally between France and Britain. Each war spilled over into the North American colonies. Most Native Americans sided with the French. The Native people hoped to keep their traditional hunting and farming regions from being settled by British colonists. Only the Iroquois became allies with the British, believing that

Fast Fact

Eighty percent of the Native population in America died due to diseases brought over by explorers and settlers from Europe beginning in the fifteenth century.

▲ Benjamin Franklin's 1754 woodcut of a snake cut into pieces was the first political cartoon published in America. The eight sections of the snake represent the individual British colonies at the time (the New England colonies are combined in one section), and the curves mimic the Atlantic seaboard of North America. The phrase beneath the snake, "Join, or Die," was a call for unity among the colonies in defending themselves against the French during the French and Indian War. Franklin's cartoon, published throughout the colonies, was based on the superstition that a snake that had been cut into pieces could come back to life if the sections were put together before sunset.

the British would eventually win and the Indians would be better off as friends of the winners.

The last of the wars finally ended in 1748, but territorial troubles between France and Britain continued. Both countries claimed land in North America that ran north to south between the Appalachian Mountains and the Mississippi and Ohio Rivers. Britain encouraged its settlers to spread westward into the territory along the Great Lakes and the Ohio River. The French and their Native American allies resisted the movement with ongoing raids along the **frontier**.

The Future of the Colonies

Some American leaders wanted to create greater unity among the thirteen British colonies, especially during the turbulent war years. The Philadelphia printer Benjamin Franklin created a plan that called for a Grand Council of leaders from all the colonies. They would oversee Indian affairs, control a colonial army, **levy** taxes, pass laws for the common good, and manage public land. All of these activities would strengthen the colonies against their common enemies. No one before Franklin had proposed that the separate colonies join together to regulate such a wide range of common concerns.

Franklin foresaw a need for the colonies to join together not only to govern, but to protect themselves against European powers seeking to take over Britain's ownership. It was obvious to Franklin and others that Britain did not have the military strength needed to prevent skirmishes with the French and Indians in the early 1750s. In addition, the colonies, all acting for themselves and without any kind of

The American Revolution

unified policy, were unable to make strong alliances with the Indians, who were needed to defeat the French if a full-fledged war developed.

Benjamin Franklin's plan for unity was presented at the Albany Congress, a meeting of representatives from seven of the British North American colonies to discuss how to have better relations with Native Americans and how to defend the colonies against the French. Franklin proposed the concept of inter-colonial self-government, an idea never before considered by colonial leaders. The Albany Plan of Union 1754, proposed that

> one general government may be formed in America, including all the said Colonies, within and under which government each colony may retain its present constitution, except in the particulars wherein a change may be directed by the said act, as hereafter follows....
>
> ...That the said general government be administered by a President-General, to be appointed and supported by the crown; and a Grand Council, to be chosen by the **representatives** of the people of the several Colonies met in their respective **assemblies**.
>
> ...That within—months after the passing such act, the House of Representatives that happen to be sitting within that time, or that shall especially for that purpose convene, may and shall choose members for the Grand Council.

Franklin's plan was quickly rejected. The king of Britain feared that the colonists would become too independent. Leaders of the individual colonies believed that the colonies would lose their power to govern themselves. This decision would prove regrettable for both Britain and its colonies. If the Plan of Union had been adopted, the colonies might have

George Washington: On the Road to Leadership

George Washington was born in 1732 and raised on a Virginia plantation. In the colonies, the wealth that a plantation provided for its owner, and the connections to colonial leadership this created, made people like Washington the equivalent of aristocrats in Britain. In 1753, at age twenty-one, he received a commission in the Virginia **militia**. That same year, Washington volunteered to deliver a message of complaint to a French commander about French **forts** being built on Virginia territory. Although the Frenchman refused to budge, Washington was praised in Britain and America for his work.

At the outbreak of the American Revolution, Washington was selected as commander of the Continental army in 1775. Congress believed that his military experience, combined with his Virginia origins (many **Loyalists** lived in Virginia), would pull the colonies together. When the colonies won their war for independence, they chose Washington, the man who led them to victory, as the nation's first president.

avoided a war, and Britain might not have lost her colonies, a valuable part of her empire.

The French and Indian War Begins

In 1744, an agreement between the Iroquois and the British gave the colonists land in the Ohio River valley. In exchange, they promised the Indians possession of land west of the Alleghenies.

British colonists hurried to establish settlements in the Ohio River valley, taking land that the French claimed was theirs. In 1749, a French representative was sent to warn the British away and enlist Native American help. When the warning went unheeded, a French officer named Charles de Langlade, who was half Indian, led about two hundred Native Americans and thirty French soldiers to destroy a major British trading post at Pickawillany in the Ohio River valley. The French then began to build forts in western Pennsylvania to protect their claims to the region.

The governor of Virginia, Robert Dinwiddie, demanded that the French leave what he called "the King of Great Britain's territories." In 1754, he sent Virginia militiamen to build a fort where the Monongahela and Allegheny Rivers meet (the site of present-day Pittsburgh). One of the militia leaders was a twenty-two-year-old lieutenant colonel named George Washington. He named the English **stronghold** Fort Necessity.

Washington's military expedition failed. French forces drove the Virginia militia out and then built their own fort, Fort Duquesne, on the site that the colonists had prepared. The conflict effectively started the French and Indian War, which spread to Europe when Britain officially declared war on France in 1756. Battles would be fought in America, Europe, Africa, the Philippines, and India in what was known outside

The American Revolution

of the colonies as the Seven Years' War (1756–1763).

The End of New France

In the summer of 1755, British general Edward Braddock led an expedition of 1,400 British troops and 450 colonials against the French at Fort Duquesne. As they neared the fort, Braddock's troops were ambushed by French and Indian fighters. Braddock and 976 of his men died in the attack. The frontier warfare continued, with the British receiving most of the damage.

In 1757, when William Pitt became prime minister of Britain, he promised the colonies that Britain would pay the expenses of raising and supporting troops if the colonists would commit in larger numbers to join the battle. Colonists joined readily, turning the tide of the war, enabling Britain to successfully defeat the French by 1760.

A New North America

The French and Indian War officially ended in 1763 with a treaty called the Peace of Paris. The treaty changed the face of North America. Britain claimed all of Canada and Louisiana east of the Mississippi River, except New Orleans. Spain gave Florida to Britain. The only land that France kept was two islands used for fishing in the Gulf of St. Lawrence and two islands on which sugar grew in the Caribbean. Following the brief period (1800–1803) during which France regained ownership of the Louisiana Territory from Spain and then sold it to the United States as the Louisiana Purchase, France's dreams of a North American empire ended. The British believed that the continent would soon be a permanent part of the British Empire. They were wrong.

▲ This painting dramatizes the retaking of Fort Duquesne by the British during the French and Indian War. In 1758, when British victory looked likely, the French retreated from Fort Duquesne and burned it to the ground rather than surrender it to their enemy. George Washington plants the British flag on what is left of the fort, reclaiming it for England.

CHAPTER 2

Trouble Brewing in Britain's Colonies

With all of eastern North America in its possession, Britain and its colonists prepared for westward expansion. Native peoples already inhabited the land to the west, though some of them had been pushed there by earlier British settlements in the east. To protect and expand the territory taken from the French and to maintain the captured French frontier forts, Britain decided to send several thousand troops to America. In this way, Britain expected to keep the Indians under control.

The cost of stationing new troops in the colonies added to the enormous war debts that Britain had accumulated in the French and Indian War. Britain's first lord of the treasury, George Grenville, decided the colonies should help pay the costs, reversing the promise William Pitt had earlier made that Britain would cover the expenses. The obvious way to collect money from the colonies was to impose taxes on them.

▲ As American settlers moved westward into Native American territory in the Ohio River valley, the Indians stepped up their attacks on remote farms, often killing the residents and burning their homes and fields.

Native American Resistance

Britain's continued military presence along the western frontier alarmed the Native peoples of the Ohio

The American Revolution

River and Great Lakes regions. Relations between the Native Americans and the British grew more hostile.

Indian warriors stepped up their raids on both the British forts and the colonial settlements. British troops were not well located to protect the isolated farms and homesteads of the frontier. Indian raiders murdered entire families, burned farms and houses, and stole cattle and food. At the same time, they fought successfully against one British fort after another. In 1763, Parliament passed a proclamation, stating that colonial governors could no longer award land grants to settlers beyond the peak of the Appalachian Mountain range. The Proclamation of 1763 appeased the Native peoples and restored some peace to the frontier.

Colonists, however, felt increasingly divided from their distant mother country. They had been poorly defended by British troops. They were faced with a law that prohibited settlement in land they dearly wanted. In addition, **Parliament** began to impose taxes that the colonists did not believe they should have to pay.

Hated Taxes

Before 1764, the colonies lived under British laws known as the Navigation Acts. Although the law did not raise money for Britain, it discouraged the colonists from trading with anybody else, including the West Indies. The Sugar Act, passed by Parliament in 1764, signaled a change. It set an import tax on molasses (a by-product of sugar-making that colonists used as a sweetener and to make rum) specifically to make money for Britain. The first paragraph of the new law stated, "It is just and necessary that a revenue [*money*] be raised...in America

▲ *The Ottowa chief Pontiac, a supporter of the French during the French and Indian War, led a short-lived rebellion against the British when colonists began settling on lands in Indian territory and the Native Americans were asked to give their allegiance to the English king. From 1763 to 1764, Pontiac's forces fought with British troops at Fort Detroit in the north, Fort Pitt in Pennsylvania, and eight other forts throughout the present-day states of New York, Ohio, Indiana, Michigan, Wisconsin, Maryland, and West Virginia. Although suffering heavy casualties, the British were finally able to negotiate a peace treaty with Pontiac's followers in 1764. The Proclamation of 1763 was a direct result of Pontiac's Rebellion.*

Committees of Correspondence

As hostility arose between Britain and its colonies, colonial leaders sought to share ideas and information and keep the colonists informed. For this purpose, in 1764, Boston formed the earliest of what would be called Committees of Correspondence.

The Boston committee's first communications encouraged other colonies to join in resisting Parliament's increasingly harsh measures. The New York Committee of Correspondence sent out word telling other colonies how New York was resisting the Stamp Act of 1765. This correspondence led to the Stamp Act Congress, a meeting of colonial delegates, held in New York City.

By 1774, nearly all the colonial legislatures had joined the network of Committees of Correspondence. Their communications built a sense of shared purpose among the colonies.

for defraying the expenses of defending, protecting, and securing the same."

The assemblies of several colonies objected to this change in policy. It would slow colonial trade, they claimed, and Britain itself would see trade with colonies decrease. Despite objections, the law remained. Colonists began to discuss resistance. Various colonies set up Committees of Correspondence in order to keep colonists aware and up-to-date on the laws and colonial reactions. This new way of communicating from one colony to the next built ties that had never existed to such an extent before.

The Stamp Act, enacted by Britain on March 22, 1765, amounted to a direct **sales tax**. Such a tax had never before been imposed on the colonies. The law required that colonists use special stamped paper, purchased from royal stamp distributors, for printing all documents. These included property deeds, newspapers, pamphlets, playing cards, almanacs, marriage licenses, and other official papers. The law had such a broad impact that no adult citizen of the colonies would go untaxed. Shortly after, in May 1765, Parliament enacted the Quartering Act, which required that colonists provide British troops in America with quarters—places to live and basic necessities. To the colonists, this sounded like taxation in disguise.

Colonial leaders throughout America reacted with outrage. The British system guaranteed that its citizens would not be taxed without their consent. The colonists were transplanted or descendants of English people and thus, as Boston leader Samuel Adams wrote, "free-born subjects, justly and naturally entitled to all the rights and advantages of the British constitution." Since their elected representatives served in colonial governments and not Parliament,

The American Revolution

the colonists believed that only the colonial legislatures could tax them.

On May 30, 1765, the Virginia legislature passed a set of **resolutions** proclaiming Virginians' right to representation before taxation. These resolutions were presented by a legislator named Patrick Henry, who declared that enforcement of the Stamp Act was "illegal, unconstitutional, and unjust, and has a manifest tendency to destroy British as well as American liberty."

In October, nine out of the thirteen colonies sent delegates to a gathering called the Stamp Act Congress in New York. Here, too, resolutions were passed that repeated Virginia's claims, calling the laws "extremely burthensome [burdensome] and grievous."

Boston's method of protest, however, proved to be the most effective. In August 1765, citizens of Boston rioted, hanging a dummy of the town's stamp distributor, burning down his office, and finally burning the dummy in a giant bonfire. The stamp distributor, Andrew Oliver, resigned his post. In one colony after another, alarmed stamp distributors did the same for fear of what the colonists might do to them, and colonists went about their business as though the law had never existed.

Colonists also agreed to a **boycott** of certain British goods, such as clothing and fine fabrics, hoping that disruption of expensive British exports would put economic pressure on the British government. Boycotts caused a drop in purchases from Britain of about 14 percent.

Under this pressure, Britain finally gave in and **repealed** the Stamp Act in March 1766. First, however, Parliament enacted a new law called the Declaratory Act. In it, Parliament declared that it had **sovereignty** over the colonies "in all cases whatsoever."

▼ Colonists protesting the Stamp Act created this stamp featuring a skull and crossbones. The image of death echoed the sentiment of John Dickinson when he wrote, "being with one mind [the American colonists] resolved to die freemen rather than to live [as] slaves."

Trouble Brewing in Britain's Colonies

CHAPTER 3

Colonial Resistance

▼ *This color print from a 1770 engraving by Paul Revere was printed and circulated throughout the colonies just three weeks after the Boston Massacre. Revere's engraving was designed to inflame anti-British feelings among the colonists. The image shows British soldiers standing and firing in an organized fashion although, in reality, shots were fired from both sides amid chaos.*

In 1767, Britain's chancellor of the exchequer (secretary of the treasury), Charles Townshend, introduced a new series of measures into Parliament. Called the Townshend Acts, these laws imposed **duties** on colonial imports of glass, lead, paints, paper, and tea.

In response to the Townshend duties, the colonists formed nonimportation associations, organized to create and enforce boycotts. The boycotts succeeded so well in reducing the importation of goods from Britain that, by 1770, the British government finally repealed all the duties except the one on tea. The colonists responded by lifting the boycotts. The tea boycott,

however, continued. Colonists turned to tea smuggled by colonial importers from Holland.

The Boston Massacre

Nowhere in the colonies were protests and anger more strongly expressed than in Boston. Massachusetts had contributed more and suffered greater losses in the French and Indian conflicts than any other colony. Everyday citizens, such as silversmith Paul Revere, made it clear that they did not like what Parliament was doing. They published articles, posters, and cartoons, gathered for rallies, and regularly harassed British officials and Loyalists. Boston inhabitants gained such a reputation in Britain for their constant agitation that soldiers were sent to the city to keep the peace.

British troops quickly made themselves unpopular by their heavy drinking and coarse language. They also accepted lower wages for various odd jobs around town, taking work away from colonists. On March 5, 1770, the very day that Parliament partially repealed the Townshend Acts, a large, unruly crowd of Bostonians gathered at the Customs House (the offices for the duty collectors) on King Street. The citizens **heckled** the soldiers on guard there and pelted them with rocks and snowballs. The gathering grew to nearly four hundred people, with those at the front yelling, "Come on you rascals, you bloody backs, you lobster scoundrels [referring to the red coats of the British soldiers' uniforms], fire if you dare...we know you dare not." It is believed that the troops' commander, Captain Thomas Preston, ordered, "Don't fire!" Even so, the soldiers opened fire, killing five men and injuring a number of others. Among those slain was Crispus Attucks, a man of African American and Indian descent, and the first black person to die in what became the American Revolution.

"Letters from a Farmer in Pennsylvania to the Inhabitants of the British Colonies"

John Dickinson (1732–1808) was an American lawyer with a strong loyalty to Great Britain, its king, and its constitution. When Parliament enacted the Stamp Act and the Townshend Acts, Dickinson responded with "Letters from a Farmer in Pennsylvania." These letters first appeared in December 1767 as a series of twelve essays in the *Pennsylvania Chronicle*.

In his essays, Dickinson set out to show how the new laws violated the British constitution. In addition, he suggested how the colonists might communicate their disagreement with the laws. He hoped that the colonists would find peaceful means to resolve their conflicts with Britain.

The letters were quickly republished in pamphlet form and circulated throughout the colonies. They led to an avalanche of petitions to Parliament and the king, as well as boycotts of the taxed items. In the process, they gave the colonists a greater sense of their unity.

In the immediate aftermath, the soldiers were arrested. British officials moved the rest of the British troops encamped in Boston to Castle William, an island fort in Boston Harbor. Pamphleteers busily informed the colonists of what they called the "Boston Massacre," and colonial leaders did all they could to heighten public reactions. "Take heed, ye orphan babes," cried Boston doctor Joseph Warren during one funeral speech, "lest, whilst your streaming eyes are fixed upon the ghastly corpse, your feet slide on the stones bespattered with your father's brains."

The Boston Tea Party

The colonial boycott of tea by now had caused tea consumption in the colonies to fall from 900,000 pounds (408,600 kilograms) in 1769 to 237,000 pounds (107,600 kg) in 1772. One company, called the British East India Company, controlled all tea trading between the colonies and India. As the company's tea continued to go unsold, the company edged closer and closer to bankruptcy (going out of business).

To prevent the company from going bankrupt, Parliament stepped in with an additional law called the Tea Act. The British East India Company would be allowed to sell tea directly to the colonists without the involvement of colonial tea merchants. Without the colonial merchants acting as tea agents and adding their own fees, the company could sell tea more cheaply than the tea smuggled from Holland.

Once again, the colonies demanded that Parliament repeal the duty on tea. The royal government refused. When boats loaded with tea arrived in colonial ports, colonists refused to unload the tea. In some cases, they sent the ships away.

Some Bostonians took resistance even further. After dark on December 16, 1773, a group of men (some dressed as Mohawk Indians) boarded three British tea ships moored in Boston Harbor. They proceeded to dump 90,000 pounds (40,860 kg) of tea overboard, an act of protest that had been carefully planned by such Boston leaders as Samuel Adams and legislator John Hancock. Lawyer John Adams later said, "There is a dignity, a majesty, a sublimity, in this last effort of the patriots that I greatly admire." The British government did not agree.

Coercion and Congress

The British government decided to make an example of the rebellious Bostonians after their Tea Party. Parliament passed a series of Coercive Acts in the spring of 1774 meant to punish the people of Boston while warning the rest of the colonies against similar behavior.

The Coercive Acts (called the "Intolerable Acts" by the colonists) closed Boston Harbor to all commerce until the town repaid the East India Company for the destroyed tea. This law put many Bostonians out of work and cut off essential supplies to the town. The Coercive Acts replaced Massachusetts legislators who had been elected by the colonists with those appointed by the king.

A new Quartering Act was also passed that applied to all the colonies. It permitted British troops to be encamped within colonial towns. In Boston, the British troops, known as redcoats, returned from Castle William, and the colony's governor

▼ *Patriots dressed as Indians hack open crates of tea, dumping their contents into Boston Harbor in the event that came to be known as the Boston Tea Party.*

Samuel Adams
(1722–1803)

Samuel Adams, pictured above, was born in Boston on September 17, 1722, the son of a wealthy brewer and cousin of the future second president of the United States, John Adams. After attending Harvard University, Samuel Adams worked as a tax collector. In 1765, he was elected to the Massachusetts Assembly.

Adams led protests against the Stamp Act, founded the secret organization known as the Sons of Liberty, and did the major planning for the Boston Tea Party. He was one of the first to propose the First Continental Congress, and he attended as one of the Massachusetts delegates. When the colonial leaders voted to declare independence from Britain, Adams joined other Patriots in signing the Declaration of Independence.

He died on October 2, 1803.

was replaced by General Thomas Gage, commander of the British army in North America.

The colonists responded to the Coercive Acts decisively. Twelve of the thirteen colonies (all but Georgia) sent delegates to a meeting called the First Continental Congress. Such a gathering that united the colonies for a single purpose had never taken place before. The delegates met in Philadelphia from September 5 until October 26, 1774. While they were discussing how to oppose the Coercive Acts and initiate another boycott, Paul Revere arrived from Boston with a set of resolutions drawn up by town leaders in Massachusetts. Called the Suffolk Resolves, the resolutions called for colonists to disobey the Coercive Acts as unconstitutional and refuse to pay all British taxes, and for Massachusetts citizens to enlist a colonial militia and engage in military training.

The Continental Congress approved the resolves and laid plans to help the people of Boston. It next approved an agreement called the Association of 1774, which urged Americans throughout the colonies to avoid using British goods and to form committees to enforce the ban. In addition, delegate John Dickinson wrote a letter from the Congress to the citizens of Canada requesting that they unite with the colonies in resisting the Coercive Acts. At the same time, he drafted a petition to King George III, asking that the king personally promote the repeal of the Coercive Acts. The petition referred to "those artful and cruel enemies [in Parliament] who abuse your royal confidence and authority for the purpose of effecting our [the colonies'] destruction."

In these ways, the American colonists faced their biggest challenge—whether to make peace with their angry parent nation or fight for the rights that they believed Britain had violated.

The American Revolution

CHAPTER 4

The Colonists' Struggle for Independence

With news of the Boston Massacre and the Coercive Acts, many Americans were finally convinced that they must fight for their rights and freedoms. In keeping with the Suffolk Resolves, men in Massachusetts gathered regularly to train as volunteer soldiers. They purchased "all kinds of warlike stores [guns and other military supplies]... sufficient for an army of 15,000 men," as voted by the Provincial Congress of Massachusetts. They stored these supplies in Concord, a village about 20 miles (32 kilometers) outside of Boston.

At the end of 1774, it was reported to Parliament that mobs had closed the king's courts in Massachusetts and forced many British officials to resign and seek protection in British forts. In February 1775, Parliament officially declared the

▼ *Colonial militiamen are fired upon by British soldiers on the town green at Lexington, Massachusetts, in the battle that marked the beginning of the Revolutionary War.*

21

Minutemen

The British colonies had their own fighting forces, called militias, long before the American Revolution. All the colonies except Pennsylvania (which was led by Quakers, who did not believe in fighting) required able-bodied men to own weapons and defend their colonies from Indian attack.

A special kind of defenders, called the **minutemen**, took up arms after Boston's trouble with the British government in 1774. They differed from militia in three ways. They were not loyal to the king, as earlier colonial militiamen (who considered themselves auxiliary British forces) typically were. They were better trained, spending more time on military drills than peacetime militiamen would do. They also agreed to be so well prepared at all times that they could gather at a minute's notice.

colonists in Massachusetts to be in a state of rebellion supported by other colonies. King George then declared that "blows must decide whether they are to be subject to this country or independent." He believed that Britain's trained troops would easily put down the amateur colonial militia. Governor Gage of Massachusetts argued otherwise. His small force of three thousand soldiers, he wrote to London, would never overcome the "fury" of the landowners and farmers of Massachusetts. Nevertheless, the king ordered him to seize colonial arms and arrest the colonial leaders of the rebellion. When Gage obeyed in April 1775, he set in motion events that would lead directly to war.

Lexington and Concord

Gage had his eye on both the military supplies at Concord and two well-known leaders of the militia, John Hancock and Samuel Adams. Hancock and Adams were staying in a village near Concord called Lexington. Gage sent out more than six hundred troops with orders to capture both **munitions** and men and bring them back to Boston.

By this time, the citizens of Boston were watching every move of the British in the city. An unidentified spy told the Americans about the king's orders and the governor's plan. The colonial leaders needed to know how the redcoats would travel to Concord, whether by a land bridge out of Boston or across the Charles River. Paul Revere agreed to signal by lantern which route the soldiers took. If the British approached by water, he would hang two lanterns in the steeple of Boston's Old North Church. If by land, he would hang only one.

On April 18, 1775, British troops launched boats to cross the Charles River from Boston. As promised,

The American Revolution

Revere signaled to the sexton of Old North Church, Robert Newman, that two lanterns should be hung in the church's steeple. Revere then galloped off toward Lexington to warn Adams and Hancock of the coming troops. Adams and Hancock escaped. By the time redcoats arrived in Lexington, minutemen had gathered on Lexington Green, the grassy town square. In the confusion that followed, a shot was fired that would later be described as "the shot heard round the world" in Ralph Waldo Emerson's poem about the event. Soon, eight colonists lay dead of gunshot wounds.

The British marched on to Concord, 8 miles (13 km) away, where they burned military supplies. On their march back to Boston, colonists shot at them with muskets. By the end of the day, seventy-two British soldiers and forty-nine colonists had fallen.

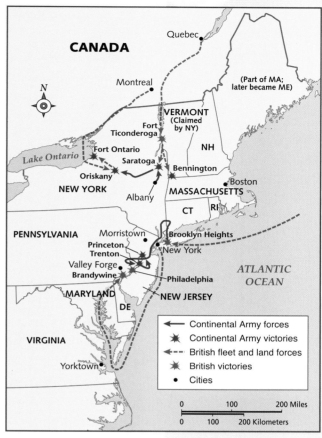

▲ This map illustrates where the early battles of the Revolutionary War took place. Continental troops were victorious in battle in New Jersey, but soon lost ground to the British in Pennsylvania. Toward the end of the war, the Continental army was able to defeat the British in the north at Bennington, Fort Ontario, and ultimately at Saratoga, which most historians consider the turning point of the war.

The Second Continental Congress

On May 10, 1775, delegates from the colonies once again convened in Philadelphia, this time for the Second Continental Congress. The delegates were more determined than ever to have control over their colonial government. They called themselves Patriots. About one-third of American colonists agreed with their point of view. Another third, called Loyalists, sided with Britain. The remaining third of the colonial population did not take sides.

In the space of a year, the Congress created an official Continental army, using the existing militia and calling for thousands of short-term enlistments by Patriots throughout the colonies. The Congress chose George Washington to lead the army. The Congress also helped various colonies sort out how they would run their governments without British involvement. It took over Indian relations, created a colonial post office, and issued paper money to purchase military supplies and keep commerce going. (Until this time, the colonies had used British currency.)

Meanwhile, on June 17, 1775, the Massachusetts militia once again faced the British army in Boston. After the conflict at Lexington and Concord, the Patriot militia had taken control of the hills surrounding Boston in order to defend the town against British assault. In June, Patriot spies brought word to militia commanders that the British planned to attack American forces on Bunker Hill. The Americans set up earthen fortifications on nearby Breed's Hill, which they believed would be easier to defend than Bunker Hill. In what became known as the Battle of Bunker Hill (it actually occurred on Breed's Hill, but was misnamed for unknown reasons), Americans successfully fought off two attacks by the British army before they ran out of ammunition and had to flee.

Toward Independence

In July 1775, the Continental Congress sent George III an official written request called the Olive Branch Petition. In it, the colonial leaders respectfully appealed to the king to stop the war and repeal the Coercive Acts. In response, the king

The American Revolution

declared the colonies to be in a state of "open and avowed rebellion." In December, the king declared all trade between merchants in Great Britain and the American colonies illegal. He also declared all American ships and their cargo fair game for takeover by the British navy. Furthermore, American crews could be **impressed** into the king's navy.

On the colonial side of the Atlantic, the royal governor of Virginia, Lord Dunmore, declared martial law, suspending the usual rights of citizens and allowing the use of military force to maintain order. Dunmore began to raise an army of colonial Loyalists who could fight alongside the redcoats, and he promised freedom to any African American slave who would leave a Patriot master and join the British. (There were slaves in all thirteen colonies at this time.) Three hundred slaves responded to his call.

In early March 1776, General Washington and his army built fortifications on Dorchester Heights, a **peninsular** hill controlling the land route in and out of Boston, and prepared to fight. British general William Howe, believing that he could no longer control Boston or fight off an attack by the

Sunday, June 18, 1775

Abigail Smith Adams described the Battle of Bunker Hill in a letter to her husband, John Adams:

> Dearest Friend,
> ...Charl[e]stown is laid in ashes. The battle began upon our [e]ntrenchments upon Bunkers Hill, a Saturday morning about 3 o'clock and has not ceased yet and tis now 3 o'clock Sabb[a]th afternoon.
>
> Tis expected they will come out over the Neck tonight, and a dreadful battle must ensue. Almighty God cover the heads of our country-men, and be a shield to our dear friends. How [many have] fallen we know not— the constant roar of the cannon is so [distressing] that we can not eat, drink or sleep.... I will add more as I hear further.

◄ Patriots at a recruiting office for the Continental army attempt to persuade colonists to fight in the war for independence.

Common Sense

Thomas Paine (1737–1809), pictured above, was an Englishman who arrived in America in 1774. His essay *Common Sense* argued convincingly that America's ties to the British crown no longer made sense. The colonies were peopled by immigrants from all over Europe. "We have it in our power," he wrote, "to begin the world over again...the birthday of a new world is at hand." Paine argued that the British king was a tyrant. "My motive and object in all my political works," he said, "...have been to rescue man from tyranny and false systems of government, and enable him to be free."

Common Sense sold over 120,000 copies in just three months, and editions were read throughout the colonies and Europe. *Common Sense* played a significant role in readying the American people for the fight ahead.

Americans, ordered British forces to leave Boston for Nova Scotia on March 17, 1776.

The Question of Independence

In the spring of 1776, news reached the American colonies that King George III had hired German soldiers, called Hessians, to help end the colonies' rebellion. The colonial leaders realized that they would now need help from a larger nation that had the military strength to meet that of Britain. Their best hope was an alliance with France, which had long been Britain's enemy. France would not deal with them, however, unless America became a nation independent of Britain.

In May, the Continental Congress approved a resolution that declared the end of British authority in the colonies. The resolution called for each colony to adopt a new government "under the authority of the people." On June 7, Richard Henry Lee, a delegate from Virginia, proposed that the Congress draft an official document stating "that these united colonies are, and of right ought to be, free and independent states; that they are absolved from all allegiance to the British crown; and that all political connexion between them and the state of Great Britain is, and ought to be, totally dissolved." Four days later, the Congress appointed a committee to produce a draft of a declaration of independence. Thomas Jefferson of Virginia was chosen to do most of the writing. The document he created adopted some of the most important ideals that were later written into the Constitution of the United States. Perhaps most important were the ideas that all people have equal rights to life, liberty, and the **pursuit** of happiness and that government exists solely for the good of the people. These ideas were gaining popularity with political thinkers of this time, and Jefferson readily applied the new theories.

The American Revolution

CHAPTER 5

Revolution!

Thomas Jefferson and his committee presented the Declaration of Independence to the Continental Congress on June 28. On July 4, 1776, after thirty-nine revisions had been made to the declaration, the Congress approved it. With this decision, the Congress finally and permanently broke the colonies' connection with the nation that had created them.

Fighting the Redcoats in 1776

Although they had retreated from Boston, the king's troops were now ordered to end the war. They could do this only by overpowering the colonists and making them obey British laws.

In August, British general William Howe and his brother, Admiral Lord Richard Howe, arrived on Long Island, east of New York City, with forty-five thousand British soldiers and sailors. On orders from the Continental Congress, American general George Washington marched south from New England with no more than twenty-eight thousand men to fight the Howes. Less than twenty thousand were adequately trained, because most had just joined the army. On August 27, the British overpowered Washington's troops.

▼ In New York City in July 1776, a mob of Patriots celebrating the signing of the Declaration of Independence pulls down a statue of King George III. Colonists later melted down the lead to make bullets for soldiers in the Continental army.

Approving the Declaration of Independence

In his autobiography, Thomas Jefferson described how the Continental Congress, **ratified** the Declaration of Independence:

Congress proceeded the same day to consider the declaration of Independence which had been reported & lain on the table the Friday preceding, and on Monday referred to a committee of the whole. The…idea that we had friends in England worth keeping terms with, still haunted the minds of many. … The debates having taken up the greater parts of the 2d 3d & 4th days of July were, in the evening of the last, closed[,] the declaration was reported by the committee, agreed to by the house and signed by every member present except Mr. Dickinson.

After losing fifteen hundred men in the battle, Washington retreated over the East River in New York under cover of a dense fog.

Through the autumn of 1776, American forces made one retreat after another, from New York through New Jersey and finally across the Delaware River into Pennsylvania. By mid-November the British had possession of the New York City region, a largely Loyalist area that was uncomfortably close to the Continental Congress in Philadelphia. By the time American forces arrived in Pennsylvania at the end of December, the Congress had fled to Baltimore.

Not until the end of December 1776 did the tide turn in favor of American forces. Washington knew that British troops were settled in a number of small **garrisons** just across the Delaware River from his troops. On the night of December 25, Washington and his Continental soldiers crossed the ice-choked Delaware River, marched to Trenton, New Jersey, and took nine hundred Hessian soldiers completely by surprise. They became Washington's captives.

On January 3, 1777, Washington led his army in a second surprise attack on a British garrison in Princeton, again taking possession of the outpost. The Continental army had badly needed the successes at Trenton and Princeton. With two encouraging victories behind them, Washington took his army to Morristown, New Jersey, where they settled in for a cold winter's wait.

On the Home Front

While soldiers fought, ordinary citizens got to work producing what the army needed. The Congress called on the colonies to keep gunsmiths busy. The Congress also encouraged gunpowder mills to keep supplies up. Iron furnaces and forges turned their work to making musket barrels, cannons and cannon balls, and huge chains for use on the ships of the Continental navy.

Other artisans were needed to meet the constant demands for clothing. Shoemakers made thousands of pairs of shoes and boots for soldiers. Farmers brought wagonloads of produce to the encamped army. Sometimes, the fighting men had plenty, but they also suffered starving times, depending on the season and the nearness of farms and laborers.

Looking Ahead

While Washington and the Continental army encamped through the winter of 1776–1777 in Morristown, New Jersey, General Howe settled his British troops in the relative comfort of New York City. Back in Britain, the king's war advisers planned for warm weather, when they could move their troops back into action. They decided to cut off New England, where the fighting had begun, from the rest of the colonies. Then they would corner the Continental troops farther south and finish the rebellion off in one decisive battle.

◀ *Colonists who could not fight still did their part to support the war. In this woodcut, gunsmiths forge guns to supply the soldiers of the Continental army.*

CHAPTER 6

The Campaign of 1777

▼ *British general John Burgoyne was forced to surrender his army at Saratoga on October 17, 1777. In this painting, the Continental forces that surrounded the British army look on as Burgoyne bows and hands his weapon over to the commanding American officer.*

In the summer of 1777, Britain's military campaign against the American colonies resumed. The plan was to cut New England off from the rest of the colonies, then proceed to an all-out defeat of Washington's troops in the Middle Colonies (New York, Pennsylvania, New Jersey, Maryland, and Delaware) before the war could move into the south.

This military campaign failed to take into account that in former wars the British had fought alongside the colonial militia against a common foe. The colonists had kept the British army supplied. In this war, all necessary supplies for the royal troops would have to be shipped from Britain and then

carried by the British troops on their campaigns. The difficulties of supplying the troops caused much delay, especially when the British troops moved inland away from the seaports.

The plan also underestimated the strong response of the colonists to warfare on their home ground. They fought not only for independence, but also for the safety of their families, farms, and businesses. Men, women, and children would take up the fight against an army that threatened their existence. In addition, Loyalists (one-third of the colonial population), whom the British had counted on for support, were fleeing the colonies due to fear of reprisals and mistreatment by their Patriot neighbors.

March from the North

General Burgoyne left Canada in mid-June with an army of about seventy-seven hundred men, including British, German, and Canadian troops and Iroquois warriors who hoped to stop the spread of colonial settlement. Traveling with them were two thousand women and children, fifteen hundred horses, and thirty wagons filled with liquor and fancy personal belongings.

Burgoyne met with early successes at Fort Ticonderoga in northern New York and in Vermont. He had intended to make his way by water to Albany, New York, but decided instead to take his huge group overland, thinking the route would be more direct. As it turned out, he lost time and supplies because his soldiers had to hack a broad path through deep forest and build bridges across creeks for their heavy wagons. Meanwhile, Americans chopped down trees to block his way, making his progress even slower and the arrival of supplies almost impossible.

The Hessians

In the 1700s, Germany was divided into hundreds of small principalities, each with its own prince. In order to raise money, these princes often hired out their young men as soldiers for other nations' wars. One such prince, Frederick II of Hesse-Cassel, provided soldiers for George III's war with his American colonies. The soldiers, known as Hessians, pictured above, were by far the largest group of German soldiers to fight in the American Revolution. Over time, Americans came to refer to all German soldiers fighting for Britain as Hessians.

As many as thirty thousand German soldiers fought in the war. In the process, they discovered communities of German immigrants, many living in German-speaking villages and towns. These German-Americans enjoyed a far better life than the soldiers had left behind in Germany. As a result, an estimated three thousand Hessians decided to switch sides in the war and remain in America.

When word spread throughout the countryside that Native American allies of the British troops had viciously murdered and **scalped** a young American woman, American militiamen turned out in great numbers. The British lost battles at Bennington, Vermont, and Freeman's Farm, New York. American major general Benedict Arnold and colonel Daniel Morgan had stopped Burgoyne's progress at Freeman's Farm (the First Battle of Saratoga, September 19, 1777). When the British tried to **counterattack** at Bemis Heights (in the Second Battle of Saratoga, October 7), Arnold led a successful charge against them. By the time Burgoyne reached Saratoga, about 10 miles (16 km) away, he knew his situation was hopeless. On October 17, he surrendered the fifty-seven hundred men who had survived the disastrous campaign to the commander of the northern Continental army, Major General Horatio Gates.

No March from the South

While Burgoyne tried in vain to follow the British plan, General Howe made plans of his own. Instead of marching north to meet Burgoyne, he unexpectedly moved his troops from New York to Philadelphia, causing the British defeat under Burgoyne. Fearful of land attacks by Washington's forces, Howe chose to travel between the two port cities by sea.

On July 23, 1777, Howe sailed with fifteen thousand men along the Atlantic coast, past the Delaware River to the mouth of the Chesapeake. He made landfall 50 miles (80 km) south of Philadelphia a month later. The Continental Congress, which had returned to Philadelphia, once again relocated, this time to Lancaster (and later to York), Pennsylvania.

Howe marched his troops north, encountering Washington's army at Brandywine Creek. He successfully broke through Continental defenses and arrived in Philadelphia on September 26. In October, British troops won another battle against the Americans at Germantown, 6 miles (10 km) north of Philadelphia, and settled in for a comfortable winter with Loyalist citizens in Philadelphia.

The French government had heard, in the meantime, of Burgoyne's surrender at Saratoga in October 1777. The French officially recognized American independence on February 6, 1778. For the remainder of the war, they would offer vital help to the Patriot cause.

A Dark Winter

With Howe and the British army in Philadelphia, Washington retreated to an encampment at Valley Forge, 20 miles (32 km) northwest of the city, with his army of eleven thousand men. The winter was notably cold and snowy, and the soldiers were poorly equipped. As many as one-quarter of the men deserted the army or died before spring.

In the meantime, much-needed help arrived from Europe in February 1778. A French military officer, the Marquis de Lafayette, was inspired by the Declaration of Independence to buy a ship and travel to America, where he stepped in to help train and drill the remaining troops at Valley Forge. At the same time, a former Prussian military man named Baron Friedrich von Steuben, who was highly trained but out of work, volunteered as well. The men of the Continental army were not professional soldiers. If they were to defeat Britain's formidable military forces, they would need to sharpen their skills as a fighting machine. Once warm weather returned, they needed to be as battle-ready as possible.

Excerpt from George Washington's Letter to Benjamin Harrison, President of the Continental Congress (Valley Forge, 1777)

Since the month of July we have had no assistance from the **quartermaster**-general ..., we have, by a field return this day made, no less than two thousand eight hundred and ninety-eight men now in camp unfit for duty, because they are barefoot and otherwise naked.... Our numbers fit for duty, from the hardships and exposures they have undergone, particularly on account of blankets (numbers having been obliged, and still are, to sit up all night by fires, instead of taking comfortable rest in a natural and common way), have decreased near two thousand men.... Although [the gentlemen of Congress] seem to have little feeling for the naked and distressed soldiers, I feel superabundantly for them, and, from my soul, I pity those miseries, which it is neither in my power to relieve or prevent.

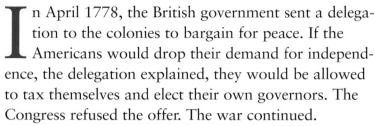

CHAPTER 7

Winning the American Revolution

▼ *A print summing up the events leading to the American Revolution–the Stamp Act, the Boston Tea Party, and the Intolerable Acts–features a* **tarred and feathered** *customs officer (tax collector) drinking from a teapot. The "Liberty Tree" with a noose symbolizes Britain's hold on the colonies.*

In April 1778, the British government sent a delegation to the colonies to bargain for peace. If the Americans would drop their demand for independence, the delegation explained, they would be allowed to tax themselves and elect their own governors. The Congress refused the offer. The war continued.

The French, meanwhile, had made their treaty with the Continental Congress, recognizing American independence. They promised that neither France nor the colonies would make peace unless they both did.

Britain now faced two foes, one on each side of the ocean. The British government had to divide its naval power to protect its interests in North America, the Caribbean, and Europe. With this new challenge in view, Britain decided to concentrate its war efforts against the colonies in the American South. There, where nearly all the colonists had family ties to Britain, the British expected to encounter the greatest number of Loyalists who would support the royal cause.

While colonial military forces continued to plan and fight, the colonial governments prepared for victory. By 1780, every state legislature had ratified a state constitution that explained how the colony would be run and what laws would govern its people. The ideas and concerns contained in these documents would later help government leaders determine what provisions to include in the U.S. Constitution.

New Life for the Patriots

With a new plan in hand, King George appointed a new commander for the British forces, Sir Henry Clinton. When General Washington broke camp at Valley Forge in June 1778 and marched against the British occupying Philadelphia, it was Clinton who evacuated British troops from the city. With them went the Loyalist Philadelphians who had welcomed the British the previous autumn.

American forces under General Charles Lee attacked the British at Monmouth Court House in New Jersey as they marched for New York City. Although Lee then panicked and ordered an American retreat (he was later punished for this move), Washington held firm. He pushed the British back to New York, but was not able to make a meaningful attack against them.

Washington waited through the rest of 1778 and 1779 for French naval support. In the meantime, British troops in the South, supported by Cherokee warriors, took Georgia with little colonial resistance in the winter of 1778.

In December 1779, Clinton divided his army, leaving enough troops to hold off Washington (now in winter quarters in Morristown, New Jersey), while taking the rest south to Charles Town, South Carolina. He took possession of the city on May 10, 1780, along with the fifty-five hundred Patriot troops defending it.

▲ Continental army and French soldiers fire upon the outnumbered British at Yorktown in October 1781. General Charles Cornwallis surrendered his army of seven thousand men when British ships, meant to reinforce his ranks, failed to arrive in the port town of Virginia that summer.

Fighting for Possession of the South

British troops defeated the Patriot forces at Camden, South Carolina, in June 1780, and British general Charles Cornwallis headed north in April 1781. After a successful sweep through Virginia (nearly capturing Governor Thomas Jefferson and other members of the colonial government), he settled in Yorktown, Virginia, to await new supplies.

In mid-August 1781, Washington finally heard that a French fleet of twenty-nine ships would arrive for a short stay off Virginia's coast in Chesapeake Bay, where Yorktown was located. Washington quickly headed south with twenty-five hundred of his troops and four thousand French troops under the French general, the Comte de Rochambeau. They were joined by other Continental and French forces, including those led by the Marquis de Lafayette.

When the British got wind of American and French movement, they rushed British ships to Chesapeake Bay, only to be overpowered by French ships already there. While the British navy backtracked for repairs, Washington approached Yorktown with fifty-seven hundred Continentals, thirty-one hundred militiamen, and seven thousand French troops.

Cornwallis surrendered and seven thousand British troops marched out of Yorktown to the sound of bands playing "The World Turned Upside Down." This British defeat signaled the end of Great Britain's fight to regain its American colonies. When word reached London of the American victory at Yorktown, British leaders chose to end the fighting. The only course left for the British government was to recognize American independence and negotiate an acceptable treaty. Peace was at hand.

The American Revolution

The End of the Revolutionary War

The French had made the crucial difference between success and defeat for the Patriots of the American Revolution. They would play a part as well in the peace treaty with Britain. The Continental Congress sent four men, called commissioners, to Paris to represent American interests in making a peace treaty. They were New York lawyer John Jay, Massachusetts lawyer John Adams, Pennsylvania publisher and inventor Benjamin Franklin, and South Carolina merchant and planter Henry Laurens.

The peace talks among the American, French, and British commissioners lasted two years. France had made its own alliance with Spain against Britain and would not make peace until Spain gained something from their common enemy. Spain received from Britain part of Florida and Gibraltar (in Europe). In addition, France would need to create its own peace treaty with Britain.

In the final treaties, signed in Paris on September 3, 1783, Britain officially recognized the independence of the United States. The treaties also determined the size and shape of the new nation. It would extend south to the northern border of Florida, which reverted from British to Spanish control, and west to the Mississippi River (except for Spanish-held New Orleans). The peace was ratified by Congress on January 14, 1784. The noble idea of a free and independent United States of America became a fact.

When Americans fought against the British at Lexington, Concord, and Breed's Hill, almost all of them still hoped to repair their relationship with their founding nation, Great Britain. Britain might have retained its colonies had its leaders understood the abilities and determination of the American people.

The Fate of the Native Peoples

During the American Revolution, Native Americans understandably mistrusted the Patriots. After all, Indian lands had been taken by the colonists again and again. A small number of Indian tribes sought friendship with the Patriots. By 1777, however, many more had taken up arms against the colonial revolutionaries.

During the war, the Congress met with Native representatives and promised to maintain boundaries beyond which white settlement would not occur. The Congress also made various alliances, promising to side with one tribal group against another. None of these promises or alliances would be honored.

At the end of the war, the region between the Appalachian Mountains and the Mississippi River became part of the United States. The Native peoples had been divided and scattered by the many battles and frequently changing alliances of the war. The Native Americans now lacked the numbers and strength to hold back the westward expansion of the white Americans.

CHAPTER 8

The War of 1812

▼ *The War of 1812 naval battle between the USS* Chesapeake *and the HMS* Shannon, *fought off the coast of Cape Ann near Boston, in June 1813, resulted in a badly needed British victory. Despite the short battle, fighting was fierce, causing more casualties than any other single-ship action in the history of both navies.*

In the years following the American Revolutionary War, the United States sought to find its place in the world of nations. In 1801, Thomas Jefferson became the nation's third elected president. He wanted the young nation under his leadership to exist at peace with other nations.

All was not peaceful in Europe, however. Britain was at war with both France and Spain. Napoleon Bonaparte, the emperor of France, controlled much of the European continent by 1805. Britain, which had the strongest navy in the world, controlled the passage of most ships at sea between North America and Europe.

The United States tried to remain neutral while Europe fought. The new country depended economically on international trade with Britain and with French and Spanish colonies in the East and West Indies, Latin America, and the Philippines. Peaceful relations with these nations promoted healthy trade.

To carry on trade with European nations, U.S. ships needed to be able to sail safely across the Atlantic Ocean. The British navy, however, made Atlantic shipping anything but safe for Americans.

New Troubles between the Old Country and the New

The royal navy needed a lot of sailors to man its ships. British officers regularly stopped U.S. ships at sea and impressed sailors from those ships into British naval service. The British officers claimed either that the sailors had deserted from the British navy or that they were actually British citizens. Many of the impressed sailors were actually former British subjects who had become U.S. citizens, so the U.S. government objected that Britain no longer had any right to take them by force. According to some reports in American newspapers at the time, the British navy had impressed thousands of U.S. citizens. To many Americans, this practice proved that Britain had not fully accepted the new nation and was trying to keep its economy from prospering.

Meanwhile, peace did not reign on U.S. soil either. White settlement in territories west of the Appalachians had raised new levels of anger in Native peoples there. Since many of the Native tribes had sided with the British in the American Revolution, bloody Indian attacks against white settlements convinced many in the U.S. government that British agents were **inciting** the violence.

The Embargo Act of 1807 prohibited all exports from American ports. Originally meant to force Britain to loosen its restrictions on American trade, the act failed to compel Britain to make changes. This political cartoon makes fun of President Jefferson's law, which was often called the "Dambargo" or "Ograbme" (embargo spelled backward). The snapping turtle, known as the "Ograbme," was used to illustrate that most merchants in the United States thought that the embargo hurt them more than it hurt the British.

The Final Steps to a New War

Relations between the United States and Britain edged toward open armed conflict when Britain passed laws in 1805 allowing its navy to seize American ships carrying trade goods from the Caribbean to Europe. As part of its war against France, Britain intercepted all direct shipping between France and its French Caribbean colonies. "Neutral" U.S. merchant ships took advantage of this policy by picking up goods in the Caribbean, stopping briefly on the mainland of the United States, then continuing to France. Many U.S. seamen became wealthy on their cut of the profits in this trade. Britain's new laws were the royal government's attempt to put a stop to it.

The United States protested in vain. As Britain suffered monumental losses to France in land battles in Europe, British interference at sea increased. To stop U.S. aid to France's shipping interests, Britain took more and more sailors from U.S. vessels and declared all "neutral" shipping in the French Caribbean illegal.

In 1807, the French responded by closing all non-British ports to British goods. In addition, Napoleon declared that any ship involved in trade with Britain could be seized. This meant that American shipping was caught in the middle of the conflict between France and Britain.

Jefferson responded with the Embargo Act of 1807, and the next president, James Madison, followed with the Non-Intercourse Act of 1809. These laws prohibited U.S. ships from leaving their home ports. American merchants who depended on international trade understandably hated the acts. Some people protested. Some seamen turned to smuggling. Meanwhile, the laws did little harm to Britain's economy and much harm in lost jobs and profits to the U.S. economy. They also worsened relations with Britain.

In 1810, Congress replaced the 1809 legislation with Macon's Bill Number Two, allowing the United States to reopen trade with both France and Britain. If only one nation promised to respect U.S. ships, the United States would favor that nation over its rival.

Napoleon responded positively. By the time Britain did the same, the American people were angry at years of what they believed to be Britain's disrespect and bad treatment. Their desire for war with Britain had become strong, and the United States rejected the offer. A group called the "War Hawks" in Congress, led by Henry Clay of Kentucky and John C. Calhoun of South Carolina, insisted that only war would preserve the nation's honor and pride.

In June 1812, President Madison made the case for war and the Senate approved it. The United States declared war against Britain for violating U.S. rights at sea and provoking the Native Americans against the United States. Andrew Jackson, a lawyer from Tennessee who served as a major general in the war, claimed that it was a fight for national honor. "For what are we going to fight?" he wrote. "... We are going to fight for the reestablishment of our national character, misunderstood and vilified [disrespected] at home and abroad."

The War of 1812 lasted for two and a half years. In the north, U.S. and British forces faced each other along the Canadian border between Lake Erie and Lake Champlain. In the south, they fought from the Florida panhandle to New Orleans. In the east, they met in the region of Chesapeake Bay.

Throughout 1813 and 1814, British ships blockaded American ports from the mid-Atlantic coast to New Orleans on the Gulf of Mexico, hoping to disrupt U.S. trade by sea. The British badgered the Chesapeake Bay region. A small force of soldiers burned most of the government buildings in Washington, D.C., including the White House and the U.S. Capitol. When British ships moved on for a full attack on Baltimore, however, the United States stood firm.

Tecumseh (1768–1813)

Tecumseh (meaning "Panther Springing across the Sky") was born in a Shawnee village in Ohio in 1768. The son of a warrior who had died in battle, Tecumseh joined his brother Chiksika in opposing white settlement of the Ohio Valley. He fought against Americans in 1782 and 1783. After the American Revolution, he participated in raids against settlements south of Ohio. In 1812, after the destruction of his family's village, Tecumseh traveled to Canada and allied himself with the British against the United States in the War of 1812.

Tecumseh's political influence among various Native tribes led to widespread Indian resistance to white settlement in the Mississippi Territory. He recruited many warriors to fight on the side of the British throughout the war. Tecumseh died in battle against American forces in Canada in 1813.

The Treaty of Ghent

Even while the British were attacking Washington and Baltimore in late 1814, negotiators were already hammering out a peace treaty between the United States and Britain to end the war. The British wanted possession of a huge piece of Maine and control of the Great Lakes. They also demanded that a state be established between Canada and the United States specifically for the American Indians.

When news of American successes in Baltimore and Plattsburgh, New York, reached London, Britain backed down. In the final settlement, the United States gained part of West Florida and a promise of peace. It met none of Britain's demands. The Treaty of Ghent was signed on December 24, 1814.

Two weeks later, a large British assault force, unaware that delegates in Paris had made peace, landed near New Orleans. The British commanders hoped that by securing New Orleans, the southernmost port on the Mississippi River, they could give Britain a strong possession to bargain with in peace talks.

U.S. general Andrew Jackson, also unaware of the treaty, delivered the decisive blow against the British at New Orleans. Jackson led forty-seven hundred U.S. soldiers, free African Americans from New Orleans, militiamen from Kentucky and Louisiana, Tennessee riflemen, and French pirates against the British. Within hours, U.S. fighters had destroyed the entire British force.

▼ The thirteen original British colonies are illustrated on this map, along with their present-day boundaries. At the close of the Revolutionary War, these colonies made up the newly independent United States of America.

New Hampshire

Massachusetts

New York

Rhode Island

Connecticut

Pennsylvania

New Jersey

Delaware

Maryland

Virginia

APPALACHIAN MOUNTAINS

North Carolina

ATLANTIC OCEAN

South Carolina

Georgia

Spanish Territory

	The Colonies
	Present-day boundaries

0   125   250 Miles

0   125   250 Kilometers

The American Revolution

The War of 1812 was a major turning point in the development of the young United States. It destroyed the military power of Native Americans between the Appalachians and the Mississippi River, opening the west to the expansion many white Americans had hoped for. Meanwhile, Americans had discovered that they were a nation of tremendous national resources. Farmers and planters took advantage of steam power to ship produce around the nation and overseas. Raw materials, such as iron and lumber, became more than goods for trade. Americans put them to good use in new factories that could produce finished products. Merchants who had earlier invested their money in shipping turned instead to U.S. manufacturing. Products such as cotton cloth called for new inventions and advanced machines that could speed up and increase production. The rise in manufacturing during the war made the nation more self-sufficient.

At the same time, the war permanently changed the political scene, leaving it open to a new alignment of leaders and ideas. The Democratic Republican Party divided into the Democratic Party and the Whig Party. The war also created two war heroes, Andrew Jackson and William Henry Harrison, who would both later become U.S. presidents (Jackson as a Democrat in 1829 and Harrison as a Whig in 1841).

Most of all, Americans reaffirmed their independence. The U.S. secretary of the treasury, Albert Gallatin, commented in this way: "The war has renewed and reinstated the national feelings and character which the Revolution had given.... [The people] are more Americans; they feel and act more as a nation."

"The Star-Spangled Banner"

In 1814, the British sailed up the Chesapeake to Baltimore after burning the U.S. capital. They intended to winter there. To take Baltimore, the British had to overcome U.S. defenses at Baltimore's Fort McHenry. Over the fort flew a huge American flag, measuring 42 by 30 feet (12 by 9 meters), that had been requested by the fort's commander.

On one of the British ships was an American prisoner named Francis Scott Key. Throughout the night of September 13, Key listened with dismay as the British bombarded the fort with rockets and bombs. At dawn, he looked toward the fort from the ship. Much to his surprise and joy, the fort still stood, with its enormous flag still flying.

Later, Key described the victory in song, writing new words to a well-known tune. In 1931, Congress passed a law making Key's song, "The Star Spangled Banner," the national anthem of the United States.

TIME LINE

1754	The French and Indian War begins.
1763	The French and Indian War ends with the Peace of Paris.
1765	Parliament passes the Stamp Act.
1767	Parliament passes the Townshend Acts.
1770	The Boston Massacre results in the first five American deaths of the American Revolution.
1773	Parliament passes the Tea Act. Colonists dump tea in Boston Harbor in the Boston Tea Party.
1774	Parliament passes the Coercive Acts. The First Continental Congress begins in Philadelphia.
1775	The American Revolution begins in Lexington and Concord. The Second Continental Congress begins. American troops inflict heavy casualties on British attackers at the Battle of Bunker Hill in Boston.
1776	Thomas Paine's *Common Sense* is published. Congress approves the Declaration of Independence.
1777	General John Burgoyne surrenders at Saratoga.
1778	France becomes an ally to the colonies against Britain.
1781	General Charles Cornwallis surrenders at Yorktown
1783	The Treaty of Paris recognizes American independence.
1784	The U.S. Congress ratifies the Treaty of Paris.
1812	The United States declares war on Britain.
1814	The Treaty of Ghent ends the War of 1812.
1815	Andrew Jackson leads a U.S. victory at the Battle of New Orleans.

GLOSSARY

allies nations associated with each other by treaty

assemblies governing bodies

boycott a refusal to buy certain goods or to buy from certain sellers

citizens people owing loyalty to and entitled to the protection of a state or nation

counterattack to attack in response to the attack of another

duties taxes charged by a government, especially on imports

forts permanent army posts stationed with troops

frontier a region that forms the edge of settled or developed territory

garrisons military camps

heckled tried to upset with name-calling and sarcastic questions

impressed forced to serve in a nation's navy

inciting stirring up

Loyalists colonial citizens who did not favor independence from Britain

levy to impose a tax

militia citizens organized for emergency military service

minutemen armed men ready to fight for defense at a minute's notice

munitions ammunition and weapons

pacifists people who are morally opposed to conflict and especially war

Parliament Great Britain's lawmaking body

peninsular projecting into a body of water and connected to the mainland by a land bridge

propaganda ideas, facts, or accusations spread to further a cause

pursuit the act of working for something

quartermaster an army officer responsible for acquiring food and clothing for troops

ratified formally approved and agreed to

repealed revoked by a formal act

representatives people elected or appointed to act on behalf of a group

resolutions formal expressions of opinion or intent voted by an official assembled group

sales tax a tax on the price of merchandise

scalped cut or torn off part of a human scalp with hair attached as a trophy of war

stronghold a fortified building

sovereignty supreme power over a population of citizens

tarred and feathered smeared with tar and covered with feathers as a punishment

FOR FURTHER INFORMATION

Books

Anderson, Dale. *American Colonies Declare Independence*. World Almanac® Library of the American Revolution (series). World Almanac® Library, 2006.

Anderson, Dale. *The Causes of the American Revolution*. World Almanac® Library of the American Revolution (series). World Almanac® Library, 2006.

DK Publishing. *American Revolution* (Eyewitness Books). DK Children, 2005.

Rappaport, Doreen. *Victory or Death!: Stories of the American Revolution*. HarperCollins, 2003.

Redmond, Shirley Raye. *Patriots in Petticoats: Heroines of the American Revolution*. Random House Books for Young Readers, 2004.

Rinaldi, Ann. *The Fifth of March: A Story of the Boston Massacre*. Gulliver, 2004.

Web Sites

AmericanRevolution.org
www.americanrevolution.org/home.html

Explore the Revolutionary Period
www.nps.gov/revwar/about_the_revolution/overview.html

Stories from the Revolution
www.nps.gov/revwar/about_the_revolution/american_indians.html

Liberty! The American Revolution
www.pbs.org/ktca/liberty/chronicle.html

Publisher's note to educators and parents: Our editors have carefully reviewed these Web sites to ensure that they are suitable for children. Many Web sites change frequently, however, and we cannot guarantee that a site's future contents will continue to meet our high standards of quality and educational value. Be advised that children should be closely supervised whenever they access the Internet.

INDEX

About the Author

Deborah DeFord has written many books about the past and its influence on the way we live today. Her first fictional book for young people, *An Enemy Among Them*, told the story of one colonial family's experiences during the American Revolution. As a writer and editor for the children's magazine *U*S*Kids*, she authored numerous articles about nature, science, and the way things work. DeFord is also the author of *Wars That Changed American History: Civil War*. She resides in Connecticut.